MAKING
MAGIC

FAY PRESTO

ILLUSTRATED BY PENNY DANN

BARRON'S

MAGIC TIPS

You are never too young or too old to start performing magic.
Try to watch other magicians work, either on the television or on stage.
You may be able to improve your own performance by learning what they
do right and what they do wrong. You may also pick up some useful chatter
or stories to tell while you do your tricks.

It is very important to be kind to your helpers and treat them with good
humor. One or two might be a little shy or nervous in front of other people.
Instead of a helper, you could use a hand puppet to help you, as Harvey the
Rabbit helps me. But you may have to change some of the tricks a little.

Although it is good to practice your show in front of a mirror, you should
also practice in front of a couple of friends before you do the real thing.

ACKNOWLEDGMENTS

Editors: Heather Amery and Anne Civardi
Designer: Anita Ruddell
Production Controller: Linda Spillane

First edition for the United States and Canada,
published 1995 by Barron's Educational Series, Inc.

First published in Great Britain in 1993 by
Hamlyn Children's Books,
an imprint of Reed Children's Books Limited,
Michelin House, 81 Fulham Road, London SW3 6RB,
and Auckland, Melbourne, Singapore and Toronto

All inquiries should be addressed to:

Barron's Educational Series, Inc.
250 Wireless Boulevard
Hauppauge, New York 11788

Library of Congress Cataloging-in-Publication Data

Presto, Fay.
    Making magic / Fay Presto ; illustrated by Penny Dann.
        p.   cm.
    "First published in Great Britain in 1993 by Hamlyn
Children's Books"—T.p. verso.
    ISBN 0-8120-9182-5
    1. Conjuring—Juvenile literature. [1. Magic tricks.] I. Dann,
Penny, ill. II. Title.
GV1548.P74   1995   94-38320
793.8—dc20   CIP
                                                     AC

PRINTED IN ITALY
5678   9933   987654321

CONTENTS

THE WORLD OF MAGIC

YUM, MY FAVORITE! CARROT.

Hello. Welcome to the world of magic that you can make happen all by yourself. I have a pet rabbit called Harvey. He got bored with just being made to disappear and reappear again, so he asked me to teach him a few tricks he could do himself. He is now very good at magic and sometimes makes me disappear.

In this book, he will show you some easy tricks and some hard ones. When I was teaching him, I gave him little presents after he had learned to do them really well. If the trick was really easy, I only gave him one carrot. Carrots are his favorite presents. If the trick was very difficult, I gave him four carrots. You don't have to like carrots to learn magic, but they show you which tricks are easy and which ones are hard.

Have lots of fun doing the magic in this book. Enjoy performing it really well, and be happy knowing you have done a good job.

ALWAYS KEEP A SECRET

Watching someone performing magic is like watching a swan swimming on the water. The swan looks as if it is gliding along without much effort. If you could look at the swan's feet, you would see them paddling hard.

When doing magic, people watching you will think it is all just happening. But you are working hard, planning ahead, setting up the next effect, and sometimes dealing with a trick that is going wrong, all at the same time.

WHOOPS!

WOW! AND NNNGH!

It is often tempting to tell people how you did a trick. The better you performed it, the more you want to tell them, and the more the people want to know.

There is, of course, no reason why you shouldn't tell them how to do it. It's a good feeling to share a secret. But several things happen when you do this.

Do you remember what you felt like when you saw a magician do a really good trick? There was a little lift in your stomach and you said, "Wow!" That's why people like watching magicians.

Do you remember how you felt when you found out how easy the trick was to do? You were disappointed and you thought, "Nnngh." When you tell someone the secret, they lose the "Wow!" and get a "Nnngh."

When you perform a trick well, really well, people clap and cheer, and tell you how clever you are. If you tell them how you did it, they may say, "That's really stupid." Keep them saying "Wow!" and thinking you're really clever.

BORING, BORING!

When you perform a trick really well, people may ask you to do it again. DON'T DO IT! The first time you do a trick, you may surprise people. The second time, they will watch more carefully and may see how to do it.

It is better to say that you NEVER repeat a trick, but, instead, you will do an even better one for them. That way, you will get more attention and applause, and be asked to perform lots of different tricks.

TESTING TRICKS

When you have practiced a trick and think you can do it well, it is a good idea to try it out on a few good friends. If they are surprised and impressed, the chances are that everyone else will be too.

A trick does not "live" until it has been performed in front of people for real. And the more you perform it, the better you will get at doing it.

FIND A CHARACTER

Some people are very funny. However hard they try, they can't get anyone to take them seriously. Other people are never funny and can never make people laugh.

Some people like wearing funny clothes. Other people just feel silly in them. But almost everyone can entertain people with magic.

The funny ones can make it very funny. They can wear outrageous clothes and add to the fun. The others can make magic much more mysterious, which will make it all the more surprising.

Find a style for yourself that is comfortable for you. Develop it and make it your own.

CHATTER OR PATTER

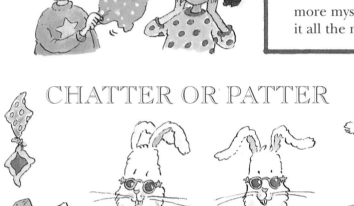

The "Chatterboxes" with many of the tricks are a guide to what you could say when you are doing a trick. The stories about a trick make the patter easier to remember and the audience will listen.

You can, of course, make up your own patter or jokes. You can make comments on something funny that has happened recently if it fits in with the trick. You can make terrible puns, particularly if you have young children in your audience. They love bad puns.

If you talk while you are doing a trick, remember not to say things like, "This is a perfectly ordinary pack of cards" or "spool of thread," or whatever you are using. It will make the audience suspicious and they will look more closely for something different and extraordinary.

ANYWHERE AND ANY TIME

A marvelous thing about magic is that you can do it anywhere. I have performed on a bus, in a submarine, on the flight deck of an airplane, and in a hot air balloon, as well as in theaters and at parties.

Sometimes I put on a formal show on a stage with curtains, lights, and a microphone. Sometimes I just do a few tricks in a restaurant or when I'm out with friends.

Magic is a wonderful thing if performed well and if you are never, ever boring.

Have fun doing it. Give everyone the chance to laugh and enjoy a mystery.

YOUR AGE IS YOUR BUSINESS

Here's a good one-carrot trick to try out on your family and friends. It's a real puzzler and no one will guess why you get the answer right every time. But never do it twice with the same people because the answer is always the same.

You'll need two notepads or pieces of paper and two pens. And you have to do the arithmetic very carefully. If you find it difficult to remember the questions at first write them down on one notepad and hand over the blank one.

I SHALL NOW PROVE I'M A MATHEMATICAL GENIUS.

THE TRICK

I NEVER ASK A LADY HER AGE.

1 Give someone a notepad and a pen. Ask her to write down on the notepad the year in which she was born. She must not tell you or let you see it written down.

THAT WAS A GOOD YEAR.

2 Now ask her to write down the year the most important thing happened in her life. Again she must not let you know what the year was or see it written down.

I'M NOT LOOKING.

3 When she has done both these things, ask her to write down the number of years since that very important event.

I'VE ADDED THEM UP.

4 Lastly ask her to write down how old she is or will be on her birthday this year. Ask her to add up all the figures but not to tell you the answer.

THAT'S RIGHT!

5 Now you multiply the year you are in by two. Write down the answer on your pad. Ask the person to show you her answer. Show her yours. They are exactly the same!

CHATTERBOX

Keep talking all the time in between asking the questions. Say things like "I was never any good at math in school. This is a really tricky one. I wish I had brought my calculator along with me." Take a bit of time while you write down your answer on the notepad. Stare very hard at it for a few seconds before you give the answer. Then say something like, "I do hope I've got it exactly right this time."

FORECASTING THE NEWS

This is a really easy one-carrot trick to start your show with. The trick is to predict what is written in a newspaper. All you need is a newspaper, a small envelope, some paper, a pair of scissors, and a pen.

Get the trick ready before the show and keep the things you need in a small box.

IN SECRET

1 Cut a thin strip of newsprint, about 1½ in. × 10 in., from the middle of a page of a newspaper. Make sure there are no pictures or large letters printed on it.

2 Carefully copy the top line of the newsprint onto a piece of paper. Make sure the words are exactly the same. Put the paper in the envelope and seal it.

CHATTERBOX
Before you cut the newspaper, move the scissors slowly up and down to keep the trick going longer. Say, "Where would you like me to stop? Here or just here, down here, or up there? Should I cut it here, here, or here? You said 'stop,' but did you mean me to cut here, here, or here?"

THE TRICK

1 Tell the audience you have made a prediction of what is written in a newspaper. Show them the small envelope you have in your hand. Give it to someone to hold and tell him not to open it yet.

2 Pick up the strip of newspaper by the bottom edge. Hold up the scissors, ready to cut the paper in half. Move the scissors up and down the paper and ask someone in the audience to say "Stop now!"

3 Cut the paper. Give the top half to someone and ask her to read the top line. Ask the person with the envelope to open it and read out loud what is written on the piece of paper. They are exactly the same!

MAGIC MONEY SPELL

Here's another good trick to do at a show or just for your friends. For this stunning trick, you need a book, eight small coins, and a helper. The book must be a hardcover book that has a little tunnel in the spine when you open it out flat. The coins should be small enough to slide in and out of the tunnel quite easily. It is best if they are all the same.

NOW FOR MY MAGIC MONEY BOOK SPELL!

THE SECRET

SLIDE IN COIN

COIN SLIDES OUT

Open the book out flat and slide a small coin into the spine. When you slide the coins out of the book into the helper's hand, the one in the spine slides out too.

THE TRICK

I'LL TAKE SEVEN COINS.

1 Ask anyone for a handful of small coins. Pick out seven, counting out loud. Make sure they are all the same sort of coins as the one you have hidden in the spine of the book.

...FOUR, FIVE, SIX, SEVEN.

2 Open the book and flip through it. Pretend to find the right page. Make it near the middle. Ask a helper to count the coins and put them in a row down the middle of the book.

HOLD OUT BOTH YOUR HANDS.

3 Very carefully close the book. Ask the helper to hold out her hands. Open the book and tip out all the coins into the helper's hands. Tell the helper to close her hands and hold onto the coins very tightly.

4 Ask another person to hold out a handful of coins. Pretend to pick one up and throw it into the first helper's hands. Ask the helper to open her hands and count out the coins aloud. She now has an extra coin.

CHATTERBOX

Start by saying, "One of the things old magicians tried to do was make money. Sorry, you can't do anything useful with magic. But this book did show me how to move money around." When you choose the coins from the helper, say: "Here are some coins. I'll take seven. One, two, three, four, five, six, seven. That's the magical mystical number." When she opens her hand and there's an extra coin in it say, "Hey Presto, the magic book did it again."

8

A WORD IN YOUR MIND

This is a good trick to do at a party or when there are lots of people in a room. You have to plan it well in advance and get it ready before the party. All you need are two books that are exactly the same. Dictionaries are the best to use. If you have one, you may be able to borrow another one from a friend or a member of your family. Or you can buy two inexpensive, identical paperbacks.

I CAN READ YOUR MIND.

THE TRICK

THIS BOOK WILL DO.

1 Tell everyone in the room that you can read their minds. Go to the bookcase or pile of books and pretend to pick out just any book. Really pick out the special book.

OPEN IT AT ANY PAGE YOU WANT.

2 Hand it to a helper. Ask the audience to agree on a page number. Then tell the helper to read out the top line of that page while you are out of the room.

I MUST FIND THE PAGE.

3 Go out of the room and close the door firmly. Quickly find the second book. Open it at the right page. Read and remember the top line of the chosen page.

AH! I THINK I'M GETTING IT.

4 Go back into the room. Ask everyone to concentrate very hard. Hold your head in your hands. Pretend to think and then say the words very slowly.

THE SECRET

Put one book in the party room where everyone would expect to see a book, such as in a bookcase or in a pile of books. Hide the other identical book outside the room where you can get it easily.

CHATTERBOX

When you start, say: "If a lot of people concentrate on a word or several words, I can read their minds. We need some words. I know, here's a book. You pick a page and I'll go outside. Someone can read out the top line. That way I won't be able to cheat." When you come back, say, "Concentrate everyone. Someone's not really trying. That's better. I'm getting it. It is…"

IN THE PACK

This is a good, easy trick to do at a show. You only need two packs of cards but both packs must have the same color and pattern on the back. Get the trick ready and keep the cards in a small box. Then they will be ready to pick up when you want them and they won't get mixed up with other card tricks you plan to do.

You can throw the cards on the floor. It looks good, but, remember, you have to pick them all up again. If you don't have time to do that, drop them onto a table or even into someone's hands.

LOOK WHAT I'VE GOT! THE TWO RED ACES.

IN SECRET

Take the ace of hearts and the ace of diamonds from one pack of cards. Put one at each end of the other pack.

CHATTERBOX

When you start the trick say something like, "Let me see now. Which card shall I choose? How about the ace of hearts and the ace of diamonds. Where are they? Come along my little red dears, no hiding in the pack."
When you drop or throw down the pack, say, "Off you all go, but I want those two red aces to stay in my hand. It's only a bit of magic."

THE TRICK

I SHALL TAKE TWO CARDS OUT OF THE PACK.

1 Pick up the pack of cards and spread them out in a fan, like this. Keep the backs of the cards towards the audience so they can't see the ace on top of the pack.

HERE ARE THE TWO CARDS.

2 Find the ace of hearts and ace of diamonds in the pack. Take them out of the pack and hold them up in your other hand. Make sure the audience can see the faces.

I PUT THEM BACK IN THE MIDDLE OF THE PACK..

3 Put the two aces very obviously back in the middle of the pack of cards. Then close up the pack and hold it firmly between your fingers and your thumb.

..AND HERE THEY ARE AGAIN!

4 Throw the pack down so that you are left holding the two outside cards. Show them to the audience. They are the ace of hearts and the ace of diamonds.

SAFE AS A BANK

In this trick there's a good story you can tell, which is easy to remember. You can think of more things to say if you want to take much longer. For the trick, all you need is a small ring. You could use a curtain ring, a metal washer, or even your mother's wedding ring. You also need a piece of string about 6 feet long, a scarf or large handkerchief, and a helper.

Practice the trick so you can take the ring off the string without looking at your hands.

CHATTERBOX
Tell this story while you do the trick. "Long ago, a rich man called Mustafa lived in the land where the palm trees grow. At that time, all the coins had holes in the middle. Mustafa looped his money onto a piece of string and tied the ends to his belt. He thought it was safe, but a clever thief sole it."

THE TRICK

I THREAD THE RING ON TO THE STRING.

HOLD THE ENDS TIGHT. DON'T LET GO.

I'LL JUST COVER MY HAND WITH THE SCARF.

1 Show the ring and string to the audience. Fold the string in half and push the loop through the ring, as shown. Push the two ends through the loop and pull them tight.

2 Hold the ring in one hand and ask the helper to hold the two ends of the string. Stand as far away from the helper as you can without pulling the string tight.

3 Pick up a scarf or handkerchief with one hand and drop it over the hand holding the ring. Put the free hand under the scarf so the audience can't see the ring.

4 Slip the string off the ring. Then ask the helper to pull the string. The empty loop comes out from under the scarf. Show the audience the ring in your hand.

THE SECRET

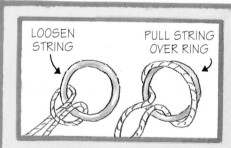

LOOSEN STRING

PULL STRING OVER RING

When your hands are hidden by the scarf, loosen the string a little and slide the loop over the ring. When the helper pulls the string, it leaves the ring behind.

ROUNDS, SHARPS, AND FLATS

All you need for this two-carrot trick is a pack of cards and a few minutes to get it ready. It's a nice and easy trick but it will really fool everyone you show it to.

Before you start, look at the numbers and letters in the top corner of each card. Some are round, like Q, others are sharp, like A, and some are flat like 7. This is the secret of the trick. With a little practice, it is easy to spot a round card, or a sharp or flat card.

TAKE HALF A PACK EACH.

FROM NOW ON I WON'T TOUCH THE CARDS.

SORTING THE PACK

Sort the pack of cards into 2 piles. Put all the cards with numbers that have round tops (2, 6, 8, 9, 10, Q) in one pile. Put the sharp and flat numbers into another pile. Then put the 2 piles together.

CHATTERBOX

Try to keep talking all the time when you are doing this trick. Say, "Just to prove it's pure magic, I won't even touch the cards. My friends here will do it all for me. Even I am surprised sometimes. It's so difficult to do. I lie awake at night wondering why it works. It's all such a mystery."

THE TRICK

HOLD ON TO YOUR CARDS.

1 Ask two friends to help you with this trick. Give one friend half the pack with all the round numbers in it. Give the other friend half the pack with all the sharps and flats.

CHOOSE A CARD FROM EACH OTHER'S PACK.

I'LL HAVE THIS ONE.

2 Ask each friend to select a card from each other's pack, to look at it and to remember it. Ask them to put the chosen card back into their own packs and shuffle them well.

3 Ask each friend to put their pack of cards face up on a table. Then ask them to spread them out, like this, so you can see all of them at the same time.

THAT'S MINE!

MINE TOO!

4 Stare very hard at each pack of cards for a moment. You can easily pick out a round card from the sharp and flat pack, and a sharp or flat card from the round pack.

BREAKFAST MAGIC

Here's a good two-carrot trick you can do over and over again and still fool your friends. You'll need two cereal boxes exactly the same shape and size, strong glue, scissors, some cereal, and a little time to prepare the trick in secret.

The trick is to show the audience an empty cereal box. After a few magic words and a bit of very clever chatter, Hey Presto, you then pour out lots of cereal into a bowl.

THIS IS A GOOD WAY TO SLIM DOWN.

CHATTERBOX

When you start this trick, try saying things like, "I'm never at my best at breakfast time, but I'm so hungry today. I really would like some cereal. Oh dear, the box is almost empty. Just one flake—that's not much of a breakfast. I'll try my magic breakfast words. Hey Presto, Hey Presto, Hey Presto. That should do it. Yes, it's worked!"

A TRICK BOX

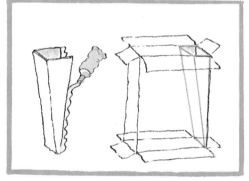

1 Open the two cereal boxes at the top and bottom, being careful not to tear the flaps. Cut a wedge out of one box about 1½ in. wide, like this.

2 Turn the wedge inside out and spread glue on the sides. Stick it inside the other cereal box, as shown. Make sure there is no gap at the bottom of the wedge.

3 Close the bottom of the box and then drop one cereal flake inside it. Put cereal in the wedge. Make sure you pack it well so it doesn't rattle. Then close up the box.

THE TRICK

SOMEONE'S BEEN EATING MY CEREAL.

IT REALLY IS EMPTY!

HEY PRESTO!

1 Open the top flaps of the cereal box, keeping the side flap firmly over the top of the wedge. Tip out the one cereal flake into a bowl. Look sad and hungry as you do it.

2 Open the bottom flaps of the box. Hold up the box with the bottom towards the audience. Show them the box is completely empty and then carefully close it up.

3 Hold up the box and tap it with one hand. Say some magic words. Then open the flaps at the top. Shake out the cereal from the wedge into the bowl.

SPLIT IN TWO

With this trick, it looks as if two pieces of rope go right through someone's waist. Get it ready in advance and put it into a box so you can pick it up when you are ready to do the trick. You'll need two pieces of soft rope, each about 4 feet long, and a piece of white or invisible thread.

IN SECRET

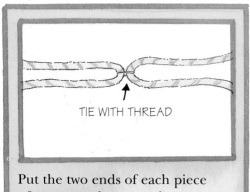

TIE WITH THREAD

Put the two ends of each piece of rope together to make two loops. Tie the two loops together with the white thread, like this. Snip off the ends of the thread.

THE SECRET

When you jerk the rope ends, the thread holding the two loops together breaks. You then pull the ropes off the helper's waist.

HERE ARE TWO PIECES OF STRONG ROPE.

I'LL TIE THE ROPES AROUND YOUR WAIST.

1 Pick up the ropes, hiding the joined loops in your hand. It should look like two separate ropes. Ask for a helper to do the trick on.

CHATTERBOX

Before you do the trick, say: "When people know you are a magician, they will always ask if you can cut someone in half. Well, I haven't got a saw and it's such a messy business. This is a much cleaner way with some rope." When you do the trick, say, "I'll tie these ropes around this brave person. Take a deep breath, now. I always thought you were much slimmer, skinny really."

2 Put the ropes behind the helper's back. Slide your hands to the ends of the rope and tie them in a knot around his waist, like this.

DID IT HURT?

3 When you are ready, give the ends of the rope a sharp tug and pull them quickly away. Hold up the loops for the audience to see.

JANGLE BANGLE

This is an easy trick to do at a show. But you'll have to practice it a few times so you can do it smoothly and easily. You need a piece of rope, about a yard long, two bangles that are exactly the same, and a felt-tip pen. The bangles must be big enough to slide easily over your hands. You also need to wear a top with sleeves that are wide enough to slide a bangle inside.

THE TRICK

1 Ask a helper to tie one end of the rope around one of your wrists, like this. Pick up a bangle and show it to the audience. Ask the helper to slide in onto the rope.

2 Ask the helper to tie and knot the other end of the rope around your other wrist. Then show the audience the bangle hanging on the middle of the rope.

3 Ask the helper to mark the knots with the felt-tip pen. This is to show that they have not been untied and tied up again. Make a big show of the pen marks on the knots.

4 Turn your back to the audience. Say some magic words and turn around again. Hold up the bangle that is off the rope and show that the rope is still tied on your wrists.

THE SECRET

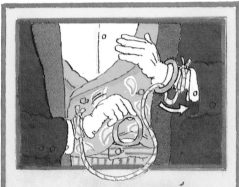

Before the show, slip the second bangle into your pocket or belt. When you turn your back, slide the bangle on the rope up your sleeve so it is hidden. Take the second bangle out of your pocket or belt and show it to the audience.

CHATTERBOX

"One of the most famous escapologists in history was a man called Houdini. This is a re-run of one of his better escapes. This bangle is Houdini. I would like this helper to imprison Houdini on this rope, by tying the ends to my wrists. We'll make sure he can't get away by sealing the knots with this black marker. Then we'll know if the knots have been untied. Let's see if he can get away. Houdini did it and I don't know how he did it."

15

CAST OF THOUSANDS

This is a card trick but it also involves the names of all your favorite film stars, pop stars, or even your school friends. You need an old pack of cards and a felt-tip pen. Write the names of the people you have chosen on the backs of the cards. Think of pairs of stars that go together, such as Tom and Jerry or Mickey and Minnie. You'll probably have to write some of the same names twice. Get the pack ready before you do the trick.

THE MAGIC IS ALL HAPPENING RIGHT BEHIND ME.

THE TRICK

I'VE WRITTEN ON THE NAMES OF FAMOUS PAIRS.

1 Pick up the pack and show the backs of the cards to the audience. Count out 12 cards from the bottom of the pack, being careful to keep them in the same order.

PUT THEM BEHIND YOUR BACK.

2 Give the first six cards to a helper. Tell her to put the cards, face up, behind her back. You put the other six cards, face up, behind your back, as well.

YOU TAKE MY CARD.

3 Ask the helper to put any card, face up, on the table. You do the same. Tell her to put your card, face down, in her pack. You do the same with her card in your pack.

AND WE HAVE A PAIR OF STARS.

4 Now ask the helper to put her cards face down on the table. You do the same. Turn over the two cards that are face up and you have both picked a pair of stars.

THE SECRET

To get the pack ready, put any 10 marked cards on the top of the pack. Count out any 10 marked cards and then put the two cards with a famous pair of names you have chosen on top of them. Put these 12 cards on the bottom of the pack. The two chosen cards are now the 11th and 12th cards from the bottom. When you give the helper a card from behind your back, always pick the sixth card. Take the helper's card and put it, face up, in your pack. Then turn over the bottom card and put it face down in your pack. This is the second of the famous pair.

CHATTERBOX

Start by saying something like this: "I've written the names of some famous pairs, and some not-so-famous pairs of stars on the backs of this pack of cards. Some of them have the same names. You know Hollywood is not what it was—not enough real stars for a whole pack of cards. And as for pop stars, I certainly couldn't think of 52 names."

FEEL THAT COLOR

This is another impressive card trick. It is even more impressive because the helper does the magic. He knows he's not a magician so you must be really magical. You ask him to feel which color the cards are and when you turn them over, he has got them all right. You just need a pack of cards, which you get ready in a stack. A stack is a few cards on the top of the pack that are in a special order.

THIS IS A VERY HOT TRICK.

THE SECRET

On the top of the pack put 13 cards in this order: red, black, black, red, red, black, black, red, red, black, black, red, red. When you show the first pair, the audience will see a black and a red card. Put them on the bottom of your pack. Show the audience the next five pairs, one at a time. Put them all back on top of the main pack. Pick up the pairs off the top of the pack. Continue until you have three cards on each marker and six on the discard pile. The 13th card is out of the way on top of the main pack.

THE TRICK

1 Silently count off 13 cards from the pack. Show a helper six pairs of cards. Take them from the front of the stack and put them at the back. Each pair is a red and black card.

CHATTERBOX
"Did you know that you can feel colors? Well, you can. Here are six pairs of cards. One card is black and one is red. I'll show them to you again but face down. Feel them with your fingers and tell me which one is red and which one is black. Does the red one feel warm and the black one cold? Wow! Clever! How did you do that?"

MARKER CARDS

2 Put them back on the top of the pack. Then take a red card and a black card from the bottom of the pack. Put them out on the table, face up. These are the markers.

3 Hold out one pair of cards, face down, and mix them up. Ask a helper to feel which is the red one. Put the chosen card face down on the red marker. Put the other one aside.

4 Do this with the next pair but ask the helper to pick the black one. Put it on the black marker. Put the other one aside. Do this with the other four pairs of cards.

5 Now turn the cards over. All the cards on the red marker are red and all the cars on the black marker are black. The pile of discards are a mix of black and red cards.

BRIGHT BANANA

In this two-carrot trick, you use what is called "magician's choice." It's a good way to get someone to choose the number you want them to from four different numbers. A member of the audience picks a number and then peels a banana. As she peels it, it falls into the same number of pieces as the number she has chosen. You need a banana that's not too ripe, a big needle, and four small blank cards.

CHOOSE TWO CARDS.

IN SECRET

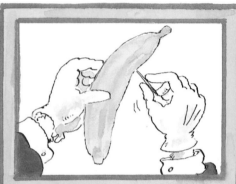

If the number you are using is 4, push the needle through the skin of the banana, about $3/4$ in. from one end. Wiggle the needle from side to side to slice the fruit inside. Try not to break the skin. Do this twice more further down the banana. Prepare the banana just before the show so the holes don't turn brown.

IN SECRET

Write four numbers on the cards. One should be 3, 4, or 5. The others don't matter. For this trick, use 1, 4, 9, and 12.

CHATTERBOX

When you start the trick, say, "I want someone to choose a number from these cards. Thank you." When you have the chosen card, say, "I had no idea what number you would choose, but this banana did. You don't believe me? Would you please peel the banana for me. Four pieces. Amazing! I don't know how that happened. It's enough to drive you bananas!"

THE TRICK

I'LL TAKE AWAY TWO CARDS.

1 Ask someone in the audience to pick any two of the four cards. If they choose 1 and 12, take them away. If they pick 4 and 9, take away the other two cards.

YOU'VE CHOSEN THE NUMBER FOUR.

2 Now ask them to pick one of the remaining cards. If they pick the 4, take the other one away. But if they pick the other one, take it away. Now you are left with the 4.

PLEASE PEEL THE BANANA.

3 Hand the person the banana and ask her to peel it. As the skin comes off, the banana splits into the same number of pieces as the number on the card she chose, 4.

THE SLIPPERY PRISONER

This is another trick with a story to tell. To do it, you need a small, colored silk scarf or handkerchief, two white handkerchiefs, a drinking glass, and a rubber band. The story is about a prisoner who can get out of any prison. The glass is the prison and the colored silk handkerchief is the prisoner. When you do the trick, it looks as if the scarf is coming out of the bottom of the glass. Tell the story as you do the trick. You can make up as much of a story as you like if you want to make the trick last a little longer.

HE'S A REALLY SLIPPERY CUSTOMER!

THE SECRET

Tie a piece of white thread to one corner of the colored scarf. Hide it in your hand. When you put the scarf into the glass, keep the thread hanging outside it.

THE TRICK

HERE IS THE PRISONER IN HIS CELL.

1 Push the colored scarf into the bottom of the glass, so everyone can see it. Push a white handkerchief, the guard, into the glass on top of it.

HE'LL NEVER GET OUT OF THERE!

2 Put the second handkerchief, which is the prison door, over the glass. Keep it in place with the rubber band. The prison door is now locked.

CHATTERBOX

This is the story: "A really slippery prisoner is put into a prison cell. A guard is put in with him. The door is shut and securely locked. The prisoner pretends to go to sleep. The guard watches him but, after many hours, he goes to sleep. Very, very quietly, the prisoner slips out of the prison cell. The door is still shut and locked. How does he get out? Well, that's a little bit of magic."

I THINK SOMETHING'S HAPPENING.

3 Hold up the glass in one hand. Put your other hand under the handkerchief and get hold of the thread that is hanging outside the glass. Gently pull it down.

THE PRISONER HAS ESCAPED.

4 Pull the thread until the scarf comes out and you can get hold of the corner. Hide the thread in your hand and pull the scarf slowly down, right out of the glass.

A PRINCELY PUZZLE

For this trick you tell a very sad story about a princess who had to marry an ugly old prince unless she could solve a difficult puzzle. To make the puzzle, you need an old playing card, a piece of string about 10 in. long, two small rings, and scissors or a craft knife. Ask an adult to help if you are going to use a craft knife.

I BET YOU CAN'T SOLVE THIS PUZZLE!

THE PUZZLE

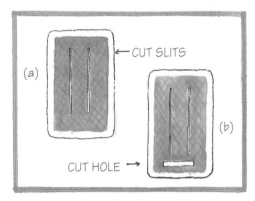

(a) ← CUT SLITS
(b)
CUT HOLE →

1 Cut two long slits in the card, like this (a). Below the slits, cut out a small hole a little wider than the slits but too small for the rings to go through (b).

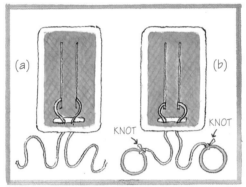

(a)
(b)
KNOT
KNOT

2 Thread one end of the string through the slits and push both ends down through the hole, like this (a). Tie one ring tightly onto each end of the string (b).

THE TRICK

WE'RE ALL WATCHING.

Give the card to someone in the audience and ask him to take the ring and the rings off the card.

Tell him he has to do it without tearing the card, cutting the string, or untying the rings from the string.

THE SECRET

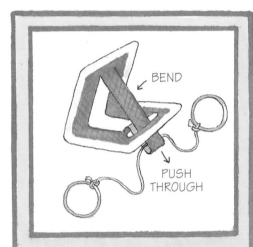

BEND

PUSH THROUGH

When everyone has given up, turn your back on them so they can't see what you are doing. Bend the card and push the strip of card through the hole. Slip one of the rings through the strip.

CHATTERBOX

This is the story: "A young and beautiful princess was told by her father, the king, that she had to marry an old and ugly prince. The only way she could escape such a horrible fate was to solve this difficult puzzle. She would then be free to marry the handsome prince she loved. Was the princess clever enough? Does this story have a happy ending?"

YOU NEED BRAINS

Here's another puzzle with a story to tell. It's about a man who wanted a wife who was clever. To make the puzzle you need two old playing cards, a ruler for measuring, scissors or a craft knife. Tell anyone trying to solve the puzzle that they have to do it in just one minute. Count slowly up to 60. This makes them hurry and think less clearly.

WHO CAN UNLOCK THIS CARD?

ME

ME

THE PUZZLE

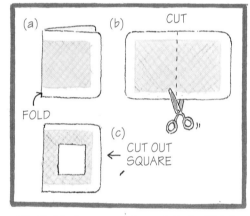

(b) FOLD

(c)

(a) CUT OUT FRAME

CUT OUT

1 Cut the middle out of one card, leaving a frame about ½ in. wide, as shown (a). Fold the middle piece in half (b) and cut out two sides, like this, to make the lock shape (c).

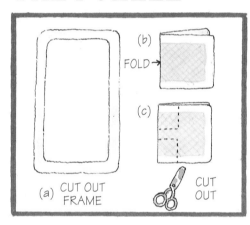

(a)

(b)

(c)

2 Fold the second card in half (a). Cut it in half along the crease (b). Cut out a square in the middle of one half, about ¾ in. across, to make a collar, like this (c).

(a) (b) CUT

FOLD

(c) CUT OUT SQUARE

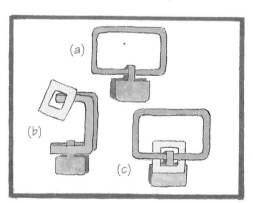

(a)

(b)

(c)

3 Fold the lock over the frame (a). Fold the frame in half. Slide the collar over the folded edges of the frame and over the lock (b). Unfold the frame and make it very flat (c).

CHATTERBOX

This is the story: "A woman wanted to marry a very handsome, charming man. But he wanted a wife who had brains as well as beauty. He agreed to the wedding on condition that she could separate the three pieces of card in one minute without tearing them. Fortunately, she had no problems and did it in under a minute. Let's see how clever you are. One, two, three..."

THE SECRET

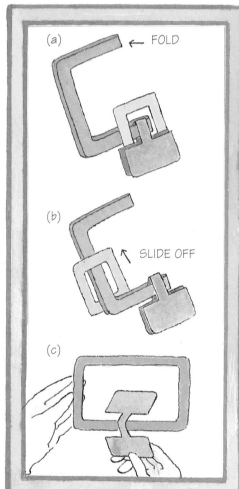

(a) ← FOLD

(b)

SLIDE OFF

(c)

To separate the bits of card, fold the frame in half (a). Slide the collar over the lock and off the frame (b). Take off the lock (c).

KNOT A ROPE TRICK

Bet your friends you can tie a knot in a rope without letting go of the ends. You can buy soft thick rope by the yard from a boat supply shop or a magic shop. Or you can buy a clothesline and pull out the center core. It is best to bind the ends with colored tape to stop them from fraying. For this trick you need a piece about a yard long.

HERE WE HAVE A KNOTTY PROBLEM.

NOW I'M IN A KNOT AS WELL.

1 When your friends have tried to tie a knot and have given up, lay the rope on a table. Fold your arms.

2 Bend over and pick up one end of the rope in each hand. Uncross your arms. And, Hey Presto, you have tied a knot.

CHATTERBOX

"Tying knots is a tricky business. There's all that stuff people tell you about left over right and right over left, but you still get in a muddle and end up with a dreaded granny knot. We magicians know all sorts of ways of tying knots and, of course, untying knots. It's not what you know, it's the way that you knot it."

DISAPPEARING KNOT

This is another quick rope trick. All you need is a piece of rope about a yard long and a shorter piece, about 4 in. long. To get the trick ready, tie the short piece around the middle of the long piece with a single loose knot. It will look like two pieces of rope tied together.

TWO ROPES TIED IN A KNOT.

WHEN IS A KNOT NOT A KNOT?

1 Pick up the rope by the two ends and show everyone the knot in the middle. Push all the rope into one hand so it is hidden.

2 Pull one end out very slowly. Keep the short piece of rope hidden in your hand, sliding it along the long piece. The knot disappears.

FRUSTRATION

The first rope trick on the facing page was kind of cheating. But this one will drive your friends crazy. You really do appear to tie a knot without letting go of the ends. Give someone another piece of rope and tell them to do exactly what you do. Get them to follow all your moves but, of course, you will forget to show them the extra secret movement you do at the end.

The instructions may look difficult to follow but once you have practiced the trick a few times, it is quite easy to do.

HELP! I'M GETTING IN A TERRIBLE TANGLE!

THE TRICK

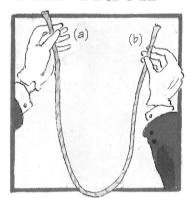

1 Hold one end of the rope in each hand. Have at least 1 or 1½ in. showing above your fingers.

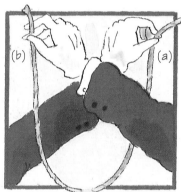

2 Put your right hand in front of your left one, so that both your wrists are crossed, like this.

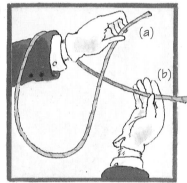

3 Then put your right hand over your left wrist and pull the rope down and out a little.

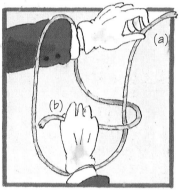

4 Bring your right hand around the loop of rope. Push it under the rope and then out again.

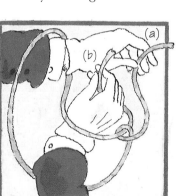

5 Pull your hands gently apart. The rope should be around both wrists and look like this.

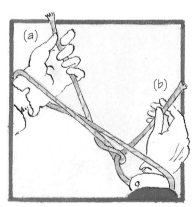

6 Hold both hands up. Drop them quickly, sliding the rope off your wrists, and you have a knot.

THE SECRET

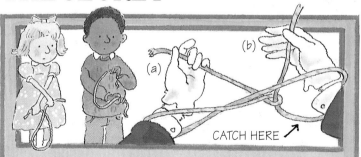

CATCH HERE ↗

When you drop your hands, let go of the end in your right hand. Quickly catch it again as the rope slides off your wrists. Make sure you have 1 or 1½ in. of end showing. Then it looks as if you held onto the rope.

MAY THE FORCE BE WITH YOU

This trick is a good way to make someone always pick the card you want them to. It's called "forcing a card." It needs a lot of practice and you have to hold the pack of cards in just the right way. When you can do it really well, no one will be able to see how it works. And you can use it for several different tricks. If you find the cards too big for your hands, you can buy packs of small-sized cards.

NOW WHICH ONE OF YOU WILL CHOOSE A CARD?

THE TRICK

1 Hold the pack, face down, in your hand, as shown, with your thumb on the top corner. You may find the trick easier to do if you fold your forefinger under the pack.

2 Run your thumb down the top corner, flicking through the pack to separate the cards. Ask someone to say "stop" and stop at that card.

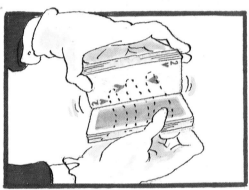

3 Open the pack, like a book, at that card with your other hand. Hold the top part of the pack with the tips of your second, third, and fourth fingers.

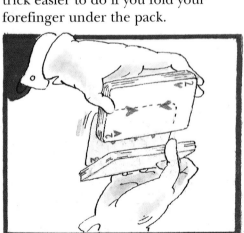

4 As you lift up the cards, help the top card to slide quietly off and fall onto the lower part of the pack. Offer someone in the audience the lower part so they take the top card.

THE SECRET

There is really only one thing you have to remember to make a forcing trick work. Before you start the trick, you must choose a card and put it on top of the pack. That is the card someone in your audience will end up choosing.

CHATTERBOX

"I'm going to flick my thumb through the pack. Just say 'stop' anywhere you like, at any card that looks good to you. Shall I stop here or here? Have you made up your mind yet? Good, there's your card on the top. Take it and look at it. Now, put it back in the pack and give the cards a good shuffle for me. What a great shuffler you are."

MORE FORCING TRICKS

I BET, I BET, I BET

In this trick you use the same way of forcing a card as you did in the trick on the opposite page. Set up the trick and ask someone to hold onto the card they have chosen. Ask them to look at it, remember it, and, without letting you see it, put it back anywhere in the pack. Of course, you know what card they chose.

1 Start to deal out the pack, face up, on the table. When you come to their card, put it down. Say "I bet the next card I turn over will be yours."

2 They accept the bet, thinking you have passed their card. Turn their card face down on the table.

FINGER ON THE PULSE

Suppose you have "forced" your helper to pick the six of diamonds. When he has put it back in the pack, say you will name it by feeling his pulse. Hold his wrist and pretend to take his pulse. Then tell him you will get it right, no matter how much he lies to you.

1 Hold the person's wrist and say, "I'll now name the four suits. Even if you try to mislead me, I can tell from the change in your pulse which is the right one."

2 Slowly say, "Hearts, diamonds, clubs, spades. It was a diamond." Call out the numbers and pictures. "Ace, two, three, four, five, six, king. It was the six of diamonds."

IN THE BOX

Before you start this trick, choose the card you are going to force. Let's suppose it is the nine of diamonds. Take the nine of diamonds from another pack of cards that looks exactly the same as the pack you are using. Put it on top of the pack and put the cards back in their box. When you do the trick, take the pack out of the box, leaving a nine of diamonds inside the box without anyone seeing it.

1 When someone has chosen their card (the nine of diamonds) and put it back in the pack, shuffle through the pack and pretend to look for it. Look puzzled and say, "Oh, dear, your card seems to be missing."

2 Shuffle through the cards again. Look as if you have had an idea and then say, "I know, it's probably still in the box." Take the card out of the box and show that it is the right one, the nine of diamonds.

VANISHING SALT SHAKER

Here's an amazing trick to do sitting down at a table. But you'll need to practice it again and again before you can do it smoothly and really astound your friends. To perform it, you'll need a small salt shaker, a coin, and a stiff linen or paper napkin.

I'M GOING TO PUSH THIS COIN THROUGH A TABLE.

THE TRICK

CHATTERBOX

Chatter all the time while you do this trick. Say, "You may not believe it, but I'm going to push this coin right through the table. First I need to find the soft spot. Every table has one. Ah, here it is. I'll cover the coin with this salt shaker and just in case the shaker breaks, I'll cover it with a napkin. Now I'll push the coin through with the salt shaker. There we are. Oh dear, the coin's still there, I'll have to try again. Oh no, not again. I'll try one more time. Whoops! Something's gone wrong, the salt shaker went through the table, but the coin stayed behind!"

NOW... WHERE'S THE SOFT SPOT?

1 Tap the coin on the table once or twice. Tell everyone you are looking for the soft spot as every table has one. After a while, pretend you have found it just in front of you.

I'LL COVER THE COIN WITH THIS SALT SHAKER.

2 Now say you are going to push the coin through the table but you have to cover it with a salt shaker first. Cover the shaker with a napkin so the shape of the shaker can be seen.

I'LL PUSH THE COIN THROUGH WITH THE SALT SHAKER.

3 Grip the shaker through the napkin and tap it on the table. Lift it towards you so that it is over your lap and clear of the table. Everyone can see the coin is still on the table.

OH DEAR! THE COIN IS STILL THERE!

4 Look disappointed and tap the shaker on the table again. Lift up the salt shaker. Again the coin is still there. Do it once again. This time, without looking at the shaker but at the coin, drop the shaker into your lap.

HEY PRESTO! IT'S GONE THROUGH.

5 Very carefully, using both hands, place the napkin, which is still in the shape of the shaker, over the coin. Let go with one hand and with a flourish bang it down hard on the napkin shape, squashing it flat.

WHOOPS! THE SALT SHAKER WENT THROUGH INSTEAD.

6 Put your hand under the table and pick up the salt shaker to show everyone that it went through the table. Say you are sorry the trick went a bit wrong and that the shaker went through the table instead of the coin.

DISAPPEARING COIN

This is a good trick to do at a show or to surprise people when they are not too close to you. All you need are two sheets of paper, about 8½ in. square, that are exactly the same. They can be white or colored but should be fairly thick. Use a ruler to fold up the paper neatly. Practice the trick a few times before you try it on anyone.

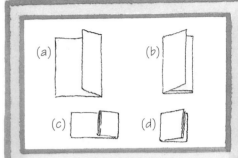

I HOPE YOU ARE A RICH BOY!

WHERE'S MY MONEY?

IN SECRET

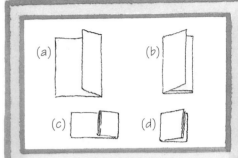

1 Fold over a third of one sheet of paper (a). Fold over the other side (b). Turn the paper around and fold over one third (c). Fold over the other edge to make a neat square (d).

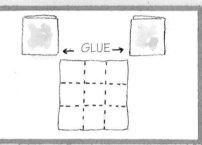

← GLUE →

2 Fold up the other sheet of paper in the same way. Glue the two parcels, back to back, with the folds on the outside. Open out one sheet of paper.

THE TRICK

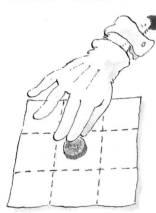

I HOPE YOU CAN SPARE THIS MONEY.

1 Ask someone for a coin. Put it in the center of the paper and fold it up neatly. Keep the paper towards the audience so they can't see the folded paper at the back.

2 Wave the paper over your head. Say a few magic words while you turn the paper parcel over. Open up the parcel and the coin has disappeared.

3 To make the coin reappear, fold up the paper and wave it around your head, turning it over. Open the parcel and the coin is there again.

CHATTERBOX

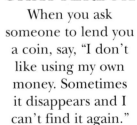

When you ask someone to lend you a coin, say, "I don't like using my own money. Sometimes it disappears and I can't find it again." After you have made the coin disappear, say, "I suppose you want your money back. Since you've been so generous, I'll see what I can do."

MAGIC WITH MIRRORS

A mirror box is a really useful piece of magic equipment to make. You'll need a small single-sided handbag mirror, about 4½ by 4 in. and thin cardboard, about 11½ by 12 in. You will also need a 45° × 45° × 90° triangle, a ruler, pencil, scissors, craft knife, and some glue. The size of the box depends on the size of the mirror. If your mirror is bigger, you can make larger things disappear but you need thicker cardboard for the box. Paint the box with colorful stripes or stars, or glue bright paper on the cardboard before you start.

A MIRROR BOX

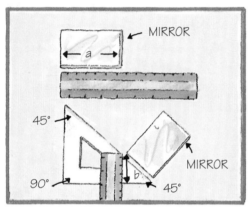

1 Measure the long side of the mirror. This is measurement (a). Hold the short side of the mirror against the long side of the triangle. Measure it straight down. This is measurement (b).

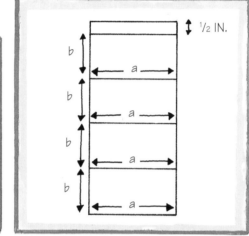

2 Now draw two straight lines down the card, the width of measurement (a) apart. Draw a line across them, ½ in. from the top, as shown. Draw three lines across, measurement (b) apart.

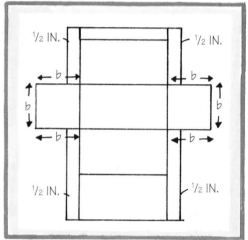

3 Draw a square on each end of the second rectangle, as shown. Their sides are each the same length as measurement (b). Draw a line ½ in. wide down the outsides of the rectangles, like this.

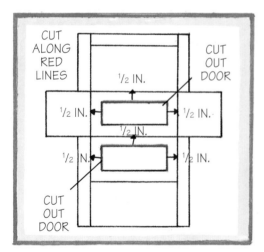

4 Draw lines, ½ in. inside all four sides of the second and third rectangles, as shown. With a craft knife carefully cut along three sides (the red lines). These are the doors.

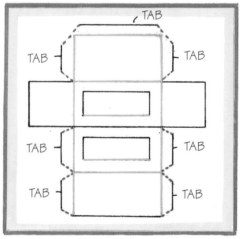

5 To make the tabs, cut along the dotted red lines. Cut out the box shape along the outside lines. Then, using a ruler and closed scissors, score along all the solid blue lines.

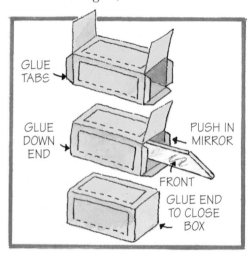

6 Fold up the four sides of the box. Glue in the tabs. Fold up one end and glue in the tabs. Now push in the mirror, diagonally, as shown. Fold up and glue in the other end.

MIRROR BOX TRICKS

VANISHING SCARF

For this easy trick, all you need is the mirror box and a small silk scarf or handkerchief.

When you do the trick, wave the box around so that the audience does not see you put the scarf in one door and then open the other one. When the scarf has vanished, you can say some more magic words and make it reappear in the box again.

I'LL PUT THE SCARF IN THE BOX.

1 Open the top and front doors to show that the box is empty Then close the front door. Gently push the scarf in the top door.

OPEN THE DOOR. LOOK, AN EMPTY BOX.

2 Close the top door. Wave your magic wand and say some magic words. Open the front door and the scarf has vanished.

BOX OF CLIPS

Here's another easy trick to do at a show. Before the show, link six paper clips together. Put them in the front door of the mirror box and close the door.

When you start the trick, be careful not to shake the box or the audience will hear the paper clips rattling inside. Or put some double-sided tape on the floor of the front door before you put the linked clips in.

DROP IN THE PAPER CLIPS.

1 Open the top door of the box and show that there is nothing inside it. Then drop six paper clips into the top door, one at a time.

AND THEY'RE ALL LINKED UP.

2 Give the box a little shake and say some magic words. Open the front door and tip out six paper clips, all linked together.

MAKE YOUR OWN WAND

A magic wand is very useful for waving over things when you say magic words. You can also use it to point to things, tap them to show they are hollow, or just to distract the audience's attention.

When you wave your magic wand, you can say "I am a mystic and this is my stick."

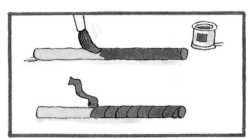

1 You will need a piece of wooden rod or dowel, about 12 in. long. Paint it black all over or wrap black tape around it very neatly.

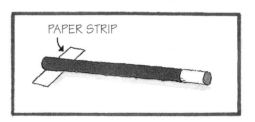

PAPER STRIP

2 Wrap a strip of white tape or white paper, about 1 in. wide, around each end of the stick. Glue it on the stick, and your wand is ready to do some magic.

SHAKE THE BOX

This trick is easy to do, but you have to get it ready in advance. You need four small cardboard boxes that all look exactly the same, four paper clips, some double-sided tape, and a rubber band.

You can keep the trick going for as long as you like by asking different people to mix the boxes and then pick the one with the paper clip.

I ALWAYS PICK THE ONE THAT RATTLES.

IN SECRET

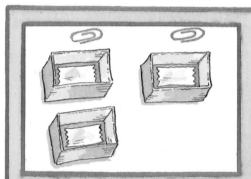

FOURTH BOX

1 Stick a big piece of double-sided tape onto the inside bottom of three boxes. Drop a paper clip into two of the boxes.

2 Drop a paper clip in the fourth box and put on the lid. Put it up your left sleeve and hold it on your arm with the rubber band.

CHATTERBOX

"I have three empty boxes and one paper clip. I place one paper clip in this box and mix up the boxes. Now, which box has the paper clip in it? This one? No, it doesn't rattle. Try another one. This one? No, that one doesn't rattle either. I'll turn my back while you mix up the boxes. I think this one has the paper clip. Yes, it rattles. And there is the paper clip."

THE TRICK

I DROP THIS INTO THE BOX.

1 Put the three boxes on the table so the audience can't see the insides. Put one paper clip in front of you. Make a show of dropping it into the empty box. Put on all the lids.

MIX THEM UP WELL.

2 Mix up the boxes. Ask someone to choose the one with the paper clip. Shake the box with your right hand. It doesn't rattle. Ask them to mix up the boxes again.

HERE IT IS!

3 Shake any box with your left hand and it rattles (because of the one up your sleeve). Take off the lid. Bang the box down hard on the table and the paper clip will fall out.

SIGNS OF THE TIMES

This trick needs a bit of practice in front of a mirror. The most important thing is to change corners without anyone noticing. You have to turn the card quickly and tell the story at the same time.

All you need is a piece of card, about 2½ in. square, which looks exactly the same on both sides, and a felt-tip pen.

Draw a black arrow on one side, pointing to the left. Turn the card over as you would the page of a book and draw another arrow, exactly the same size, but this time pointing downwards.

THESE ROAD SIGNS ARE VERY CONFUSING.

THE SECRET

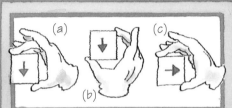

If you hold the card by two opposite corners and rotate it, the arrows point the same way (a). When you hold the opposite corners and rotate it, one arrow points one way, the other points the other way (b). Change corners, the arrows point up and down (c).

THE TRICK

YOU SEE THIS
THE AUDIENCE SEES THIS

1 Hold up the card between your thumb and middle finger by two corners, as shown (a). When the arrow on your side points down, the arrow on the audience's side points left (b).

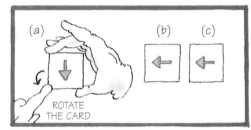

ROTATE THE CARD

2 Still holding the card between your finger and thumb (a), begin the story. Turn the card around. The arrow points to the audience's left (b). Do it again. It still points left (c).

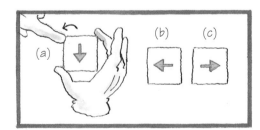

3 Cover the card with your other hand. Change your finger and thumb to the other two corners (a). Turn it around and the arrow points to the audience's left (b). Turn it again and it points to their right (c).

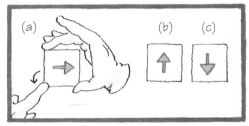

4 Cover the card and hold the other two corners so the arrow points to the right on your side (a). Turn the card around and the arrow points up on the audience's side (b). Turn it again and it points down (c).

CHATTERBOX

This is the story. "A man got a job painting road signs. His boss told him to paint signs with arrows on both sides, pointing to the left, like this. Soon his boss came up and said, 'There was a mistake. You should have painted the arrows on the other side, facing the other way. Otherwise, all the cars coming the other way would turn left and not right.' 'That's no problem,' said the man, 'I'm a magician. I wave my hand and the arrows on the back turn around.' 'That's very good,' said his boss, 'but can you help us when the road is repaired and the traffic can go straight?' 'No problem,' said the man. 'I wave my hand and the arrow on the back of the sign will say 'Go straight.' "

COPY CAT TRICK

Here is an incredible three-carrot trick to play on one of your friends. You'll need two packs of playing cards with exactly the same cards in each pack.

You'll amaze your friend when you choose the same card from your pack as he does from his. The secret is to remember the bottom card of your pack before you give it to your friend.

LOOK, WE'VE CHOSEN THE SAME CARD!

WOW! THAT'S BRILLIANT.

THE TRICK

CHOOSE THE PACK YOU WANT.

1 Put both packs of cards on a table. Then ask your friend to pick up one of them. Pick up the other pack yourself.

2 Start shuffling your pack and ask him to do the same to his pack. Make a big show of how you shuffle your cards.

I MUST REMEMBER THE BOTTOM CARD.

3 Change packs with each other. As you give him your pack, very secretly look at the bottom card. Remember this card.

4 Tell your friend to fan out his cards and pick one. You do the same. Both look at your cards without showing each other.

5 Each put your card back on top of your own pack and then cut the packs wherever you like. Now swap packs.

HERE IS THE CARD I REMEMBERED.

6 Ask your friend to find his card in his pack. Then find in your pack of cards the card that you remembered at the start.

7 Pull out the card next to it on the right. Now both turn your cards over. Hey Presto, they will be exactly the same.

CHATTERBOX

It is a good idea to distract your friend's attention while you are doing this trick. The best way to do this is to ask him to copy everything you do! Perhaps you could scratch your nose, pull on one of your ears, or blink your eyes.

A ROPEY TRICK

Astound your friends by turning three pieces of rope, all different lengths, into three pieces all the same length. It takes lots of practice and a bit of very clever chatter to do this ropey trick really well.

You can use any kind of rope or thick string, or you can buy a special soft rope from a magic shop.

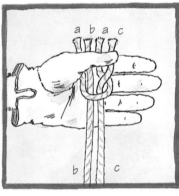

I START WITH THREE DIFFERENT LENGTHS OF ROPE.

...AND TURN THEM ALL INTO THE SAME LENGTH.

THE TRICK

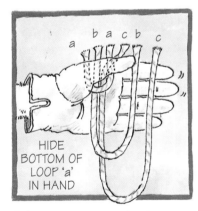

1 Cut a long piece of soft rope into three separate pieces, about 10 in. long, 22 in. long, and 36 in. long.

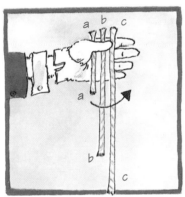

2 Hold the three pieces of rope in your left hand, between your first finger and your thumb.

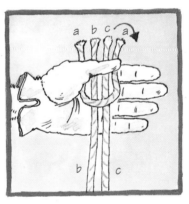

3 Take the free end of the shortest piece of rope and loop it up in your hand, as shown.

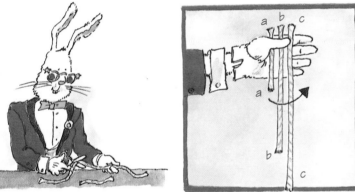

4 Then twist it under the longest piece, like this. Try to do this bit without anyone noticing.

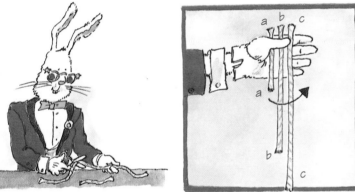

HIDE BOTTOM OF LOOP 'a' IN HAND

5 Now take up the free ends of the other two pieces, one at a time, and hold them in your hand, like this.

6 Loosely hold three ends of rope in your left hand and the other three ends in your right hand, as shown.

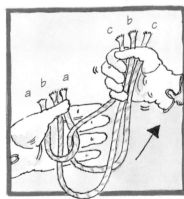

7 Slowly pull your hands apart keeping the loop hidden in your left hand. You will see that all three ropes are the same size.

CHATTERBOX

"In my left hand I have three pieces of rope, one short one, one medium one, and one long one. I loop them all up, one at a time, like this. Will someone please blow hard over the ends for me? That's just right. Hey Presto, now the ropes are all the same size!"

TUBE TRICKS

For these two amazing three-carrot tricks you'll need some magic tubes, a small plastic cup, a silk scarf, and some food coloring. You can make the magic tubes yourself out of thick paper or cardboard.

Practice the tricks over and over again before you perform them and remember to chatter all the time.

HERE ARE TWO TUBES.

THERE'S NOTHING IN THIS ONE...

MAKING THE TUBES

PLASTIC CUP

CUT OFF RIM

(a)

(b) (c)

10 IN.

CARDBOARD

1 Cut the rim off a small plastic cup (a). Straighten out a paper clip (b) and tape it to the cup (c).

2 To make the small tube, cut out a piece of cardboard 10 in. long. Roll it loosely around the cup, like this.

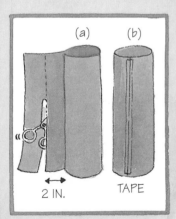

(a) (b)

2 IN. TAPE

SMALL TUBE

BIG TUBE

3 Cut off the extra cardboard, leaving about 2 in. (a). Overlap the edges. Tape them to make tube (b).

4 Make another tube slightly wider than the first. Make sure the small one slides into it.

DOWN THE TUBES

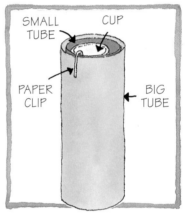

SMALL TUBE CUP

PAPER CLIP

BIG TUBE

HIDE PAPER CLIP

PUSH IN SCARF

1 Before you start, slide the small tube inside the big tube. Put the plastic cup inside the tubes with the paper clip looped over them, as shown.

2 To perform the trick, cover the paper clip with your thumb. Wave a small silk scarf in front of your audience. Then push the scarf down the tubes into the plastic cup.

WATER SURPRISE

FOOD COLORING

1 Before you start this trick, put a drop of food coloring or a bit of instant coffee into the bottom of the plastic cup.

2 Put the plastic cup into the empty tubes with the paper clip looped over both tubes. Cover the paper clip with your thumb.

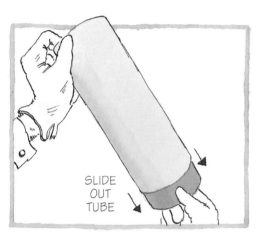

SLIDE OUT TUBE

3 Tap the tubes with your magic wand and say some magic words. Then, holding the paper clip firmly between your finger and thumb, slide the small tube down out of the big one. Show that it is empty. Put it back.

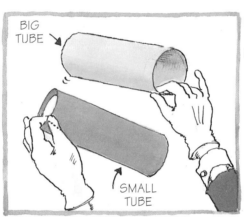

BIG TUBE

SMALL TUBE

4 Now slide the big tube down from the small one and show the audience that it too is empty. The paper clip holds the cup inside the small tube as the big tube is removed. It is very important that they do not see the paper clip. Then slide the big tube back over the small one.

5 Ask someone in the audience to tap the tubes for you with your magic wand. Then whisper some magic words into the top of the tubes. With a big flourish pull the silk scarf out of the magic tubes.

3 Show the audience that both tubes are empty in the same way as you did in the last trick. Don't let them see the paper clip.

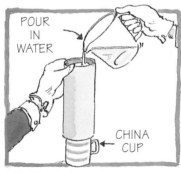

POUR IN WATER

CHINA CUP

4 Hold the tubes over a cup and pour some water into the tubes. No one will know it is going into the plastic cup.

WATCH OUT!

EMPTY CUP

5 Pick up the cup and pretend to throw the water over your audience. They will be amazed to see that there is no water.

LOOK! IT'S A DIFFERENT COLOR.

6 Say some magic words and pour the water out of the plastic cup into a glass. Hey Presto, look, it's changed color.

THE UNBEATABLE SPOOFER

Baffle your friends with this amazing three-carrot coin trick. It needs lots of care and a little practice to perform it like a real magician. The trick is to knock a coin through a helper's hand into a wine glass. As well as the glass, you'll need a big coin and two small ones exactly the same. Try a few coins out to see which ones work best.

I'M GOING TO KNOCK THIS COIN THROUGH YOUR HAND.

CHATTERBOX

When you start the trick, you can say, "This is a very, very difficult trick. I've got to push a coin through your hand into a wine glass. I hope I don't make a hole in your hand. Well, here goes." When you hit the bottom of their hand with the second small coin say, "One, two, three, Hey Presto, look there are two coins in the glass. Phew! I didn't make a hole in your hand either."

THE TRICK

I'LL SLIP THIS COIN INTO THE WINE GLASS.

1 Hold one of the small coins under the big one so that nobody can see it. Slip them down the side of the wine glass so they rest on the bottom.

LOOK, IT'S MOVING IN A CIRCLE!

2 Swirl the wine glass around. You will see that the small coin stays under the big one and it looks as if there is only one coin in the glass.

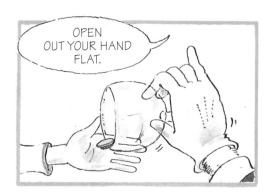

OPEN OUT YOUR HAND FLAT.

3 Carefully pour the two coins out of the glass onto your helper's hand. Quickly cover them with the glass. Pick up the second small coin and show it to the audience.

1, 2, 3 HEY PRESTO!

4 Hold the second small coin by your fingertips and move it up and down under the person's hand. Hit the bottom of their hand with the second small coin.

THE SECRET

HE'S BRILLIANT!

When you hit the person's hand, the coins in the glass jump up to show two instead of one. If they land together, look puzzled and hit the person's hand again. While everyone is peering into the glass looking at the two coins, quietly stand back and casually slip the second small coin in your hand into your pocket.

CUTTING THE ROPE TRICK

For this trick you need a piece of thin, soft rope, about a yard long, a short piece of rope, about 4 in. long, and a pair of scissors. The scissors should have points and be sharp or you will have trouble cutting the rope.

This is a good close-up trick as long as you hide the extra piece of rope in your hand really well. Keep the rope and scissors in a box, ready to do the trick. You'll need the box at the end of the trick too.

WILL YOU PLEASE CUT THE ROPE FOR ME?

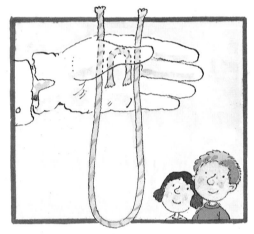

1 Make the short rope into a loop and hide it in your hand, as shown. With the back of your hand towards the audience, hold the long rope by your thumb so that both ends show.

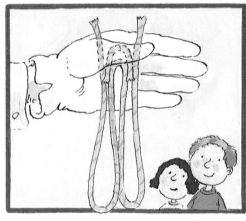

2 Pick up the long loop of rope and put it in your hand so that it doesn't show above your fingers. Tuck it under your thumb just below the short loop of rope, as shown.

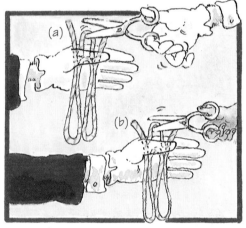

3 Push one point of the scissors under the short loop of rope. Pull it gently upwards so that a loop shows above your fingers (a). Ask someone to cut the loop of rope (b).

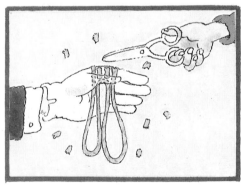

4 Pull the two ends of rope up a bit and ask someone to cut them off to make them look neat. Let the cut ends and the short pieces left of the small loop fall to the ground.

IT'S STILL IN ONE LONG PIECE.

5 Now ask someone to pull the rope on the left hand side out of your hand. As they marvel that it is still in one piece, put the scissors into the box and take a bow.

CHATTERBOX

When you do this trick, say: "This is a very useful piece of magic. If someone cuts a long piece of rope in half, you can just say the magic words and join them back together again. Of course, you have to say the right magic words. Just any old words won't work. Magic is a very ropey business. Sometimes it works and sometimes it doesn't. I'm not stringing you along!"

WE HAVE CONTROL

This is an easy trick to do once you have gotten the knack of it, but you will need to practice it several times before you can do it really well. The point of the trick is to secretly shuffle a chosen card from the top of the pack down to the bottom and back up to the top again. When you can shuffle a card about, keeping it under your control, you can do the amazing trick on the next page, like a real magician.

I'M GOING TO GIVE THE CARDS A REALLY GOOD SHUFFLE.

THE TRICK

PLEASE REMEMBER YOUR CARD.

1 Ask a helper to select a card from a complete pack of cards. Ask him to look at it and place it, face down, back on the top of the pack.

WOW! THAT'S MY CARD.

2 Shuffle the pack of cards really well. Hold the pack out to the helper and ask him to turn over the top card. It is the chosen card.

CHATTERBOX

"Just put your card back on top of the pack. Thank you. Now I'll shuffle the cards really well. I'll go on shuffling until you say 'stop.' We could go on all night if you've already forgotten the magic word. Did you say 'stop'? Good! Now turn over the top card and look at it. Hey Presto, it's the card you chose. That's real magic for you!"

THE SECRET

1 When the chosen card is on top of the pack, hold the deck in one hand, as shown here. The thumb of the other hand slides the top (chosen) card off.

2 As you lift up the deck, let the chosen card fall into your hand and quickly drop the other cards over it. Shuffle the pack, leaving the chosen card at the bottom.

3 At the last shuffle, pick up the bottom few cards. Let them slide on top of the pack, one on top of each other, making sure the chosen card falls last, making it the top card again.

THE AMAZING LIE DETECTOR

You can lie, tell the truth or both, but this trick will always find you out. It is done in the same way as you did the control method on the opposite page.

I KNOW IF YOU ARE TELLING THE TRUTH!

THE TRICK

I'M NOT LOOKING.

1 Ask a helper to choose a card from the pack, to look at it and show it to the audience without letting you see it. Then ask her to put it back on the top of the pack.

TELL ME WHEN TO STOP SHUFFLING.

2 Shuffle the cards, slipping the chosen card to the bottom of the pack. At the last shuffle, move the card to the top with two cards on top of it. Take the top nine cards without changing their order. Use *only* this stack of cards for the trick.

T.H.R.E.E.

3 Ask the helper to give you the number of the card she chose. She can lie or tell the truth. Deal the cards from the top of the stack, one card for each letter of the number, say T.W.O. Deal them down on top of each other, reversing their order.

C.L.U.B.S.

4 Without changing their order, put the cards back on the bottom of the stack. Deal two cards for the word of —O-F. Put them on the bottom of the stack. Deal cards for each letter of the suit, say C-L-U-B-S. Put them on the bottom.

THAT'S REALLY YOUR CARD!

5 Ask the helper if the card she named was true or lies or both. Deal the letters of the word she chooses, say L-I-E-S. Turn over the next card of the stack of nine cards and it is the chosen one.

CHATTERBOX

"This is not just a pack of cards, it's also a lie detector. You can lie or tell the truth or both. It doesn't matter. The lie detector will find you out. Now, let's spell out your card. Was it a number or a picture card? Ah, a ten? T-E-N. It was the ten of something—O-F. Of what? Spades, clubs, diamonds, or hearts? Ah! clubs—C-L-U-B-S. Was it lies, true, or both? Ah! Both. B-O-T-H. Your card was the ten of diamonds."

DICEY DICE

Here is a four-carrot trick with three dice. It needs a little bit of practice and lots of concentration to get the knack of making it work every time. You need three dice that are the same size. Dice about $\frac{1}{2}$ in. square are best. If you don't have any dice, you can try using sugar lumps instead.

IS THERE MAGIC IN YOUR FINGERS?

THE TRICK

NO, JUST DROP THE MIDDLE ONE.

1 Put the three dice down on a table. Then ask someone to pick them up between her thumb and forefinger.

2 Now ask her to drop the middle die but still keep hold of the two other dice on either side.

THE SECRET

HOW DO YOU DO THAT?

3 The magician, of course, does it quite easily. The middle die drops down and the other two dice snap together, like this.

CHATTERBOX

When you do the trick, try saying something like, "We magicians have to move very quickly. The speed of the hand deceives the eye, or so they say. This is a little exercise we perform to see if your fingers are quick enough. I'll just hold the three dice like this and say my magic words. Hey Presto, just look at that. Away goes the middle die. It's as easy as can be!"

Before you pick up the dice, secretly lick your finger and thumb. Press them firmly onto the dice. Open them quickly and let the middle die slip out, before closing them again.

CATCH AS CATCH CAN

For this trick you need two dice and a glass or cup. Challenge your friends to hold the dice against the side of the glass and catch them, one at a time, in the glass without losing the first one out of the glass. It sounds easy and looks easy. It isn't. Do the trick first and ask them to do it. Even if they watch you very carefully, both catches look so much the same, when they try it, they won't be able to do it.

THIS REALLY IS A DICEY TRICK.

THE TRICK

1 Hold one die against the side of the glass with your first finger. Then carefully balance the second die on top of it, as shown.

2 Gently flick the glass upwards so that the first die is tossed in the air. Quickly catch it in the glass. That one is the easy one to do.

3 The second die needs a little more practice. You have to let go of the die and, at the same time, move the glass quickly down.

IT'S ALL A MATTER OF SPEED!

4 Catch the die as it falls. Go on moving the glass down a little way and then go more slowly until it stops with both dice in it.

CHATTERBOX

When you do the trick, say, "Here is another exercise we magicians have to do to check the lightning speed of our reflexes. It's simple but effective. First I toss one die in the air and catch it in the glass. Well, that's the easy part. Then, this is a little trickier. Hey Presto, I cleverly catch the second die without the first one flying out, just like this!"

THE AUDIO-VISUAL TACTILE ILLUSION

This is a good four-carrot trick to do as the last one in your show. You can make it funny or create a very mysterious atmosphere. The finish is spectacular. You break a length of cotton thread into several short pieces and magically they put themselves back into one long piece. All you need is a spool of thread and a pencil.

NOW FOR SOME THREAD MAGIC!

THE SECRET

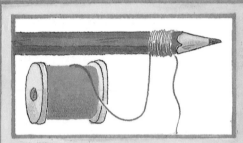

1 Pull off about 2 yards of cotton thread from the spool. Hold the spool and pencil as shown. Wind a yard of thread around the pencil.

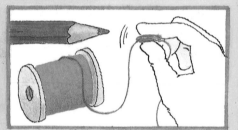

2 Lick the finger and thumb of your other hand and slide the thread off the pencil. Pinch the bundle flat as it comes off, like this.

3 Roll the bundle back along the thread towards the spool. Wind the thread a few times around the bundle. Let the end dangle down.

4 Hold the bundle against the spool. Wind the thread tightly around it once to hold it on the spool. Then wind it once around the spool.

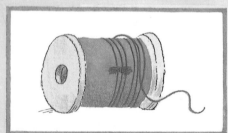

5 Wind the thread three or four times around the spool, avoiding the bundle. Wind on the rest of the thread. The trick is now ready.

CHATTERBOX

"I'm going to do an illusion with 2 yards of thread. Did you hear that break? It didn't break at all. It was an illusion of the ear. It was an audio illusion. Did you see that break? It didn't break at all. It was a visual illusion. Would you break this thread into short pieces? Thank you. Did you feel the break? No. It was an illusion of touch. A tactile illusion. Keep going. That's it. May I have all the pieces back, please? Thank you. Now I'm going to create the illusion that they are all one piece. There, a long piece with a big bundle in the middle. Not convinced? O.K. I'll hang the bundle a little nearer the middle. There, could you take that end? Thank you. Very gently now. I don't want this bundle to fall off and spoil the illusion. Now, very gently, pull it apart. Wow!"

THE TRICK

1 Pick up the spool with your forefinger and your thumb, covering the bundle with your thumb, like this. Everyone will think you are showing there's no trickery.

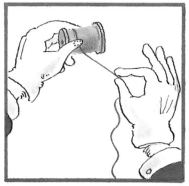

2 Unwind the thread. You will feel it slide under your thumb. Then it will just unwind. As you feel it under your thumb again, get ready to collect the bundle.

3 As the thread comes off the spool, follow it with your thumb. When the bundle comes off, pinch it between your forefinger and thumb so no one can see it.

4 Hold the spool with the forefinger and thumb of your other hand. Hook your little finger around the thread between the bundle and the spool, as shown.

SHORT THREAD

LONG THREAD

5 Break the thread about 4 in. from your finger and thumb. You now have a short thread and a long thread. Give the end of the long piece to a helper.

6 Ask the helper to break it into short pieces. Take back the pieces and hold them with the tips of the finger and thumb that is holding the bundle.

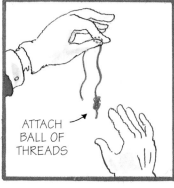

ATTACH BALL OF THREADS

7 Take all the pieces, except the one with the bundle, and roll them into a ball with your other hand. Press the ball onto the bundle thread, close to the end.

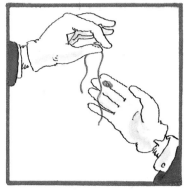

8 Leave the ball dangling on the thread for a couple of seconds and then take it off with the other hand. Say that you need to move it up a little.

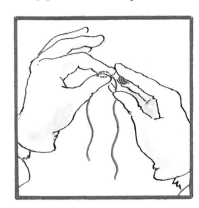

9 Pretend to move the ball of thread up, but really hide it between your first and second finger, like this. Make sure nobody sees you doing it.

10 Pick up the dangling piece with that hand. Very gently let go of the bundle in the other hand, as if you were afraid it would fall off the thread.

11 Give the dangling end to a helper to hold. Pick up the other end in the other hand, still hiding the short pieces between your finger and thumb.

12 Ask another helper to hold the other end. Ask the two helpers to pull the thread very gently apart. The bundle will slowly untangle.

PUTTING ON A SHOW - 1

In this book there are several types of tricks for you to perform. Some work best when you are sitting at a table, some when you are standing up in front of a crowd, and some are just puzzles. A mixture of them will make a very good magic show.

ARE YOU READY FOR SOME MAGIC?

IT AIN'T WHAT YOU DO, IT'S THE WAY YOU DO IT

It is important to remember that whenever you do magic, you are putting on a show. Even when you are sitting at a table with two friends, it is still a show. The show should be long enough to entertain but short enough not to be boring.

Three or four tricks performed really well are better than ten done badly. If a trick doesn't entertain your audience, it doesn't matter how difficult it is. If it does entertain them, it doesn't matter how simple it is. Your costume, the music, if you are using it, and what you say are just as important as the tricks you do.

THE SHOW

Before you put on a show, look at where you are going to perform it. If it is a large space with lots of people, choose tricks that look good from a distance. Avoid the ones that work well in close-up.

MUSIC

Some magicians prefer to do a "silent act." This means they do not speak but do a few tricks to music. Not really a "silent act." This may seem an easy way of performing but it can be quite hard. The magic has to fit the music and the music fit the magic.

You have to hold the attention of your audience when not a lot is happening. And once the music has started, everything has to go very smoothly. You can't stop and start again if things go wrong. It takes a lot of practice to get it absolutely right.

Tricks that work well silently are "Down the Tubes," "A Ropey Trick," "Water Surprise," "Cut and Mend," and "The Mirror Box."

TALKING OR "PATTER"

Some magicians are good at words and talking to people. Chatting to people they don't know is easy for them.

A "patter" or "live act" is one where the performer talks to the audience. The performer must know the tricks well and be able to concentrate on the audience. This needs a little more experience and a little less practice.

The only way to get the experience is to put on a show.

Some tricks work well when sitting at a table with friends. The magic can be very unexpected. You have to plan ahead, although it shouldn't look as if you have. Many of the card tricks in this book work well at a table and also in a patter act.

WOW!

HELPERS AND ASSISTANTS

For some of the tricks, you need a helper. You can either ask a friend to come to a show with you or you can ask for a helper from the audience.

If you ask for a helper from the audience, try to pick someone who looks quite different from you. It is best to pick someone who looks as if she is having fun.

When the trick is over, thank her for her help. If the trick went really well, you can ask the audience to give her a clap and tell the helper to take a bow. Then, with a flourish, show her back to her seat.

If you ask a friend to help you, she can stand at the side, ready for when you need her. Or she can sit at the front of the audience and be ready to volunteer quickly when you ask for a helper. You then pretend it is someone you don't know.

A friend who really wants to be your assistant can be very useful. You can practice with the friend, plan the show together, and may even think of ways of improving the tricks. A funny friend may be able to make a joke or two if a trick goes wrong. She can also try to distract the audience if you get yourself in a mess.

WHAT TO WEAR

What you wear is more important than you may think. A costume, even if it is just a cloak and a hat, can make you feel special.

If you are doing a few tricks at a table, don't rush off and come back in a hat. But some handy pockets can make all the difference to a smooth performance, especially if you go on to more tricks. You can dress up as a clown, or as a witch or a wizard. Or you can wear a party dress, a special bow tie, or just your best clothes. You need pockets, a belt, or loose sleeves for some tricks.

Whatever you put on, make sure they are clothes that are comfortable and you feel happy wearing. They should be clean and well pressed, even if they are casual clothes.

The more amazing you look, the more fascinated your audience will be. And your costume may help to distract their attention when you do a particularly difficult trick.

MAKING MISTAKES

If a trick goes a little bit wrong, don't worry about it. If you haven't given away the secret, you can either say, "Well, let's try that one again and hope to get it right this time." Or you can go on quickly to the next trick.

PUTTING ON A SHOW - 2

WHERE TO PERFORM?

You can perform anywhere. That is one of the great things about magic. If you are doing a show in a room full of people, look around first. Try to choose a place in the room that has a focus. A fireplace is good. By a door is sometimes useful for entrances, and exits when the show is over.

Try not to perform in front of windows. You want the light to shine on you, not from behind. Some rooms have French windows with long, thick curtains. These can give you a little theater. If you can arrange to have a screen or a blank wall behind you, there are fewer distractions for the audience to look at. Then they will only look at you and your magic.

When performing in a room with the curtains drawn and the lights on, try to have a light near you. A standard lamp close to your table, with the other lights turned off, will make your space look more like a theater.

If you need a table for your tricks, ask someone to help you move it to the best place. A table looks better if it has some kind of cloth or cover on it.

If you are using music, find out where you can plug in your tape player or radio. Try to have it close to where you are performing so you can turn it on and off easily.

When you are putting on a show that will last for more than ten minutes, try to have enough chairs for the audience to sit down. They will be much more relaxed and ready to enjoy themselves.

Young children can sit on the floor, on cushions, in front of the chairs. This will stop them from running about and interrupting your magic performance. Before you start, tell them that it is very important for them to keep quiet.

BEFORE THE SHOW

Before a show, plan all the tricks you are going to do. Write them down in a list and make sure that no two tricks are too alike. Make them all as different as possible and put a quick trick in between two longer ones.

Only put in tricks you can do really well and have practiced lots of times in front of one or two friends. Start with a quick, dazzling trick and save your best one until last so you end on a great finish.

For the first and last tricks, choose ones that don't need a helper. This gives you a quick start, and an ending when you take the applause on your own and can bow your way out.

I'M READY FOR SOME MAGIC.

SHORT BUT GOOD

Don't try to do too many tricks in a show, especially if you haven't much experience. An audience may not like magic as much as you do and may get bored. A short, very good show is better than a long, not-so-good one.

BE PREPARED

Get ready any tricks that need to be prepared in advance, such as a stack of cards. Put all the things you need—the cards, scarves, dice, pieces of equipment—in the same order as your list. Then they will be in the right place for you to pick up in the right order during the show.

IN THE RIGHT ORDER

It is a good idea to put all your equipment in a box to take to the show. If you have a second box, you can put the tricks in it after you have done them. Then you won't get confused and the audience won't be able to look at your equipment.

Take your list with you to the show. Put it down where you can see it to remind you which order you plan to do the tricks. You can then move smoothly from one trick to the next.

PRACTICE

Practice all the tricks again before the show. Wear the clothes that you will wear for the show. Then you will be able to use the pockets, belt, or sleeves when you need them.

Always choose the magic you really enjoy doing. Then there is a good chance the audience will enjoy it too. Good luck and have fun.

WHERE DO WE GO FROM HERE?

When you can do some of the tricks in this book really well and have put on a few shows to entertain your friends, you may want to learn more about magic.

MAGIC CLUBS

Joining a magic club can be fun. Most large towns in most countries have magic clubs for people over 18 years old. They also often have junior sections.

ASK THE PROFESSIONALS

If you have a party, or go to one, and there is a magician to entertain you, try to have a quiet word with him after the show. He may be helpful.

If not, do not give up. Look in the classified telephone directory for magicians and telephone one or two. Eventually, you will find one who will be happy to help you.

MAGIC SHOPS

You may find a list of magic shops in the classified telephone directory. They are worth visiting, but some of the salespeople may seem rude at first. Keep trying and they will probably be very nice when they know you are really serious about magic.

Many shops also have a mail order service. Be careful. Sometimes the descriptions of a trick can be misleading, so don't be too eager to spend lots of money. Some cheap tricks can be very good. Some expensive ones are very boring.

It is sometimes best to buy a trick you have seen performed. Then you know it works and you may be able to spot how to do it.

NEW TRICKS

Once you have learned some magic, you may be able to invent some tricks of your own. Or you can make changes to old tricks or do them in lots of different ways.

This works very well at a magic show. The audience may have already seen some of the tricks you do. But if you have a surprising ending, they will give you extra applause.

Always be on the lookout for ways of improving your magic. You can learn from other magicians and from books. You may have an idea to make a very simple trick into a longer and more complicated one by adding an extra twist to it and lots of chatter.

HAVE LOTS OF FUN AND GOOD LUCK!

The best advice I ever had was given to me by a great Italian magician, Arturo Brachetti. He said: "There is a moment when you do the trick and a moment when you do the MAGIC. When you do the trick, keep all the little movements that make it work very small."

Then, taking a deep breath and standing up really straight, Arturo said: "Ah, but when you do the MAGIC, then you make all your movements very large and very grand."

THANK YOU ARTURO!